Little Book of

PARTERRE AND KNOT GARDENS
IN FRENCH KNOTS

Little Book of

PARTERRE AND KNOT GARDENS
IN FRENCH KNOTS

Christine Harris

SALLY MILNER PUBLISHING
(MILNER CRAFT SERIES)

*D*edication

FOR JOHN, WITH LOVE

First published in 2001 by
Sally Milner Publishing Pty Ltd
PO Box 2104
Bowral NSW 2576
AUSTRALIA

© Christine Harris 2001

Design and diagrams by Anna Warren, Warren Ventures, Sydney
Edited by Sue Stravs
Printed in Hong Kong
Photography by Sergio Santos

National Library of Australia Cataloguing-in-Publication data:
Harris, Christine, 1947–.
    Little book of parterre and knot gardens in french knots

    ISBN 1 86351 282 9.

    1. Embroidery. 2. Embroidery - Patterns. 3. Painting. I. Title
    (Series : Milner craft series).

746.44

Disclaimer
The information in this instruction book is presented in good faith. However, no warranty is
given, nor results guaranteed, nor is freedom from any patent to be inferred. Since we have
no control over the use of information contained in this book, the publisher and the author
disclaim liability for untoward results.

Contents

ACKNOWLEDGEMENTS

I would like to thank the companies that kindly donated the threads used in the following projects. Ristal Threads (Canberra) for the Au Ver a Soie, DownUnder Australia (Sydney) for the Waterlilies and Radda Pty Limited (Sydney) for the DMC threads.

Mary, Mary quite contrary

How does your garden grow?

With silver bells and cockle shells

And pretty maids all in a row

NURSERY RHYME

Introduction

My fascination with French Knots began many years ago and has not decreased with time. I love this little knot because it is such a versatile and simple stitch. The more I use it, the more applications I can find for it.

French Knots are perfect to depict the formality of parterre and knot gardens. I have thoroughly enjoyed working these projects and hope the reader might use these outlines, most of which are based on traditional garden designs of the 17th century, to create their own individual pieces. Try experimenting with different colours and threads to create your own unique pieces.

Happy stitching.

. . . .

My gardens sweet, enclosed with walles strong,

Embanked with benches to sit and take my rest

The knots so enknotted, it cannot be exprest,

With arbours and alleys so pleasant and so dulce,

The pestilent airs with flavours to repulse

UNKNOWN 16TH CENTURY POET

Basic Requirements

FABRICS

All the projects in this book have been worked on calico or very fine Irish linen. As the embroidery covers the entire surface of the design area, your choice of these fabrics is optional. Calico works well because it is very closely woven and the tiny knots do not pull through.

Before you begin your embroidery, I suggest you wash the fabric well, to remove any dressing. Iron the fabric while it is still damp.

THREADS

Stranded embroidery floss and fine silk threads are ideal for this type of embroidery. Work in short lengths of about 30 cm (12 inches). Longer thread becomes very worn and will not give you a professional finish. Silk is particularly prone to wear when longer lengths are used. Always strip the stranded thread, that is, separate the strands before use.

NEEDLES

For this type of embroidery, I prefer to use a crewel needle. If using a single strand of embroidery thread, I always use a size 10 needle. Some embroiderers find this fine needle difficult to thread. However, please persevere, it is worth the effort to achieve tiny knots.

Use a size 10 needle for a single strand of thread, size 9 for two strands and size 8 for three strands.

EMBROIDERY HOOPS

Use a small hoop. The ideal size is just large enough to hold the design. Keep the fabric tension very tight. If using a wooden hoop, bind the inner ring with cotton tape. Do not leave your work in the hoop when not in use as it may damage the fabric.

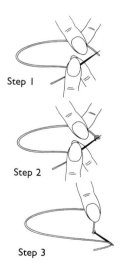

Step 1

Step 2

Step 3

General Techniques

All embroidery is worked using single twist French Knots. All projects are worked on a 20cm (8inch) square piece of fabric.

TRANSFERING THE DESIGN

Using a sharp 2B lead pencil and your preferred light source, lightly trace the design onto the fabric, taking care to keep the straight lines of the design on the grain of the fabric.

Please note: all the design outlines are actual size.

A separate border may be worked to complement the design. The shape, width and colour is a matter of individual preference.

OUTLINING A DESIGN

When instructions call for the design to be outlined, work a line of French Knots, using the same motion as when working back stitch. Bring the needle up at A, form the knot, take the needle down at B, bring the needle up at C, form the knot, take the needle down at D, bring the needle up at E, form the knot, take the needle down at F. Continue in this manner, working the knots closely together. See Diagram 1.

E   F C   D A   B

Diagram 1

STRAIGHT STITCHES

When working the tiny straight stitches, bring the needle up through the worked knots and take it back down almost through the same hole so that just a hint of colour is showing.

HINTS

Always use an embroidery hoop. Place the fabric into the hoop and stretch until taut. Tighten the hoop, using a screwdriver if necessary.

Always knot your thread before beginning to stitch. When working the French Knots, be careful not to take the needle back through the hole you created when the needle came up through the fabric.

When instructions are given to fill the area, that area is filled with single twist French Knots.

LAUNDERING

I recommend laundering all embroideries prior to framing. Gentle hand washing in warm, soapy water using pure soap is suggested. Rinse very thoroughly to remove all traces of soap. Do not wring the fabric. Roll in a clean towel to remove excess moisture. To press, place the damp embroidery right side down on a clean white towel. As the knots are massed very closely together, heavy pressing is not necessary. Hold a stream iron just above the embroidery and gently steam. Press the fabric surrounding the embroidery. Stretch, being careful to keep the fabric square, and pin to a surface such as an ironing board to dry completely.

THREADS

DMC Stranded Cotton:
470 (avocado green)
471 (very light avocado green)

937 (medium avocado green)
Waterlilies by Caron: 'Eggshell'

The design is worked throughout in single twist French Knots using a single strand of thread.

Hedges

Outline the entire design with 937, as described in Outlining a Design in General Techniques. Using 471, fill all the hedges with closely worked French Knots. Then, using 470, scatter some knots on top of those already worked. If you prefer a lighter shade of green, do not work this darker shade too closely together. If you would prefer a darker shade, work more knots of this colour through those already worked.

Paths

Fill the paths with 'Eggshell'. Do not work the knots too densely, they should barely touch.

One should cultivate letters or his garden.

VOLTAIRE

THREADS
DMC Stranded Cotton:
211 *(light lavender)*
470 *(light avocado green)*
471 *(very light avocado green)*
472 *(ultra light avocado green)*

522 *(fern green)*
927 *(light grey green)*
3346 *(hunter green)*
3363 *(medium pine green)*
3364 *(pine green)*
Waterlilies by Caron: 'Eggshell'

The design is worked throughout in single twist French Knots using a single strand of thread.

Hedge 1

Outline the shape with 3346, as described in Outlining a Design in General Techniques, and then scatter a few knots of this colour through the area. Fill almost half the remaining area with 3363. Fill any spaces still left with 3364.

Hedge 2

Outline the hedge as before, using 470. Then scatter a few knots of this colour through the area. Complete as for Hedge 1 using 471 and 472.

Hedge 3

Fill the five circular areas using equal numbers of knots in 522, 927 and 211.

Paths

Fill the paths with 'Eggshell'. Do not work the knots too densely, they should barely touch.

· · · · · · · · · · · · · · · · ·

Yes, in the poor man's garden grow

Far more than herbs and flowers —

Kind thoughts, contentment, peace of mind,

And joy for weary hours.

MARY HOWITT

ANNE'S KNOT GARDEN

THREADS
DMC Stranded Cotton:
209 (dark lavender)
211 (light lavender)
340 (medium blue violet)
341 (light blue violet)
522 (fern green)
543 (very light beige brown)
550 (very dark violet)
602 (medium cranberry)
603 (cranberry)

604 (light cranberry)
727 (very light topaz)
739 (very light tan)
746 (off-white)
972 (deep canary)
973 (bright canary)
3051 (dark green grey)
3347 (medium yellow green)
3348 (light yellow green)
3746 (dark blue violet)
white

The design is worked throughout in single twist French Knots using a single strand of thread.

Hedges A and B
Outline the shapes with 3347, as described in Outlining a Design in General Techniques. Fill the hedge areas with 3348.

Area 1
Fill a little more than half of each area with 604. Scatter equal numbers of 603 and 602 to fill the areas. Finish by scattering a few 3051 through the knots already worked.

Area 2
Leave a small, unworked border around the edge of each section.

Using single strands of 209, 211, 340, 341 and 3746, fill the centre of each section with a mixture of colours in any combination. Scatter a few 3051 through the knots already worked.

Fill the remaining unworked border with equal numbers of knots in white and 746. Using 522, work a few tiny straight stitches through the border flowers, as described in General Techniques.

Area 3
Leave a small, unworked border around the edge of each section.

Fill the centre of each section using 973 and then scatter approximately four or five knots using 972. Work approximately five green knots through the flowers using 522.

Using 211, fill a little less than half the unworked border. Fill all the remaining spaces with 727 and then finish by scattering five or six knots using 550 through the border flowers.

Paths
The paths and a narrow area (approximately 3mm or ¼ inch) surrounding the garden are worked with equal numbers of knots in 739 and 543. Do not work the knots too densely, they should barely touch.

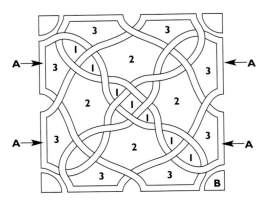

$\mathcal{E}$MMA'S KNOT GARDEN

THREADS

Au Ver a Soie, Soie d'Alger:
531 *(very pale lemon)*
2123 *(very light olive green)*
2124 *(medium olive green)*
2125 *(olive green)*
3013 *(rose)*
3021 *(light rose)*
3723 *(pine green)*

4111 *(beige)*
4911 *(light blue violet)*
4912 *(medium blue violet)*
4913 *(blue violet)*
white — *optional, see Outlining
    Garden Beds*
DMC Stranded Cotton:
3770 *(very light flesh)* — *optional,
    see Paths*

The design is worked in single twist French Knots, with some straight stitch.

The thread is used in single strands throughout.

Hedge 1
As described in General Techniques, outline the hedge using 2125. Fill most of the circle with this colour, then fill any remaining spaces with 2124.

Hedge 2
Work as for Border 1, using 2123 and then 2124. When the lines intersect in the centre of the design, work the darker colour as the predominant shade for each line that travels OVER. Then, using 2125, work two short straight stitches at the edge of the outline. These straight stitches should be only two or three knots long. Take care to work in the correct direction to emphasise where the lines cross over.

Hedge 3
Work as for Border 1, using 2124 and then 4911.

Garden Bed 4
Using 3013, scatter six to eight knots. Fill the remaining area with 3021, then scatter a few knots using 3723.

Outlining Garden Beds
Work a single row of white knots around the edge of Garden Beds 5, 6, 7 and 8.

This step is optional and the design works equally well if you choose to eliminate the white edges.

Garden Bed 5
Work three knots in each corner with 3021. Fill the centre of the section with 531, then scatter a few 3723.

Garden Bed 6
Work clusters of knots through each bed using 4911, 4912 and 4913. Fill the remaining space with 531 and a few knots in 3723.

Garden Bed 7
Work as for Garden Bed 4.

Garden Bed 8
Using 4912 and 4913, fill most of the remaining area, then scatter a few knots in 3723.

Paths
Using 4111, work a circle of knots around the design. If you feel this colour is a little dark, you can lighten it by scattering some knots in 3770 through those already worked.

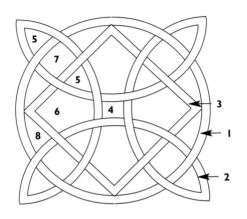

My lovely garden too adjoining lies,
Of sweetest flowers, and of the richest dyes:
The tulip, jas'min, emony, and rose,
Of which we'll garlands for thy head compose.

AYRES

ELIZABETH'S KNOT GARDEN

THREADS

DMC Stranded Cotton:

211 (light lavender)	3052 (medium green grey)
340 (medium blue violet)	3053 (green grey)
341 (light blue violet)	3347 (medium yellow green)
522 (fern green)	3348 (light yellow green)
734 (light olive green)	3362 (dark pine green)
744 (pale yellow)	3363 (medium pine green)
746 (off-white)	3364 (pine green)
818 (baby pink)	3688 (medium mauve)
819 (light baby pink)	3689 (light mauve)
927 (light grey green)	3819 (lime)
	white

The design is worked throughout in single twist French Knots, with some straight stitch. Use a single strand of thread unless otherwise specified.

Garden Bed 1

Using one strand of 3362 blended with one strand of 3363, fill most of the circle with closely worked knots. Work more knots on top of those already worked to give a domed appearance.

Garden Bed 2

When working this section, leave a narrow unworked border around the outer edge.

Using two strands of 818, work three clusters consisting of 8-10 knots. These clusters should be more or less evenly spaced.

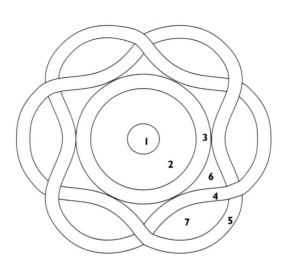

    With one strand of 340 blended with one strand of 341, work five clusters of approximately seven knots, evenly spaced in the area. Using this same combination, scatter some knots at random.

    Using one strand of 3053 blended with one strand of 744, work two knots closely together in about eight places. Blend one strand of 3688 with one of 3689, scatter approximately 35-40 knots through the area. Then, using two strands of 744, work three knots next to those just worked.

    Scatter knots at random through the section using two strands of 818.

    Fill any remaining spaces with equal numbers of single strand knots in 3052 and 3363.

Now fill the unworked border with tightly massed knots in white. With a single strand of 3347, work tiny straight stitches scattered at random through these flowers, as described in General Techniques.

Lavender Hedge 3

Blend together one strand each of 927 and 522 and fill almost half the area. Then, using one strand of 927 blended with one of 211, fill the remaining area.

Hedge 4

Using one strand each of 3363 and 3364 blended together, fill the area, taking care where the lines pass over and under the interlocking shape.

Hedge 5

Using two strands blended together in any combination of 734, 3819, and 3348, fill half the area. Then blend one strand each of 3348 and 3364 to fill the remaining area.

Garden Bed 6

Blend one strand each of 340 and 341 and work about seven or eight knots in a circle. Then, depending on the space available, work one, two or three knots on three sides of the flower in 3364. Fill the remaining outer edge with single strand 746.

Garden Bed 7

Using two strands of 818, work a cluster of about seven knots in the centre of each section, then work a cluster of three knots on both sides of the 'flower'. Using a single strand of 3053, work some knots to represent 'leaves' on both sides of each of the three flowers. Fill the remaining area with equal numbers of single strand knots in 819 and 746.

$\mathcal{E}$LEANOR'S PARTERRE GARDEN

THREADS

DMC Stranded Cotton:
340 (medium blue violet)
523 (light fern green)
744 (pale yellow)
745 (light pale yellow)
778 (very light antique mauve)
819 (light baby pink)

3688 (medium mauve)
3689 (light mauve)
3747 (very light blue violet)
3756 (very light baby blue)
ecru
white
Waterlilies by Caron: 'Blush'

The design is worked throughout in single twist French Knots. Use a single strand of thread unless otherwise specified.

Outline the garden bed edges with 523, as described in Outlining a Design in General Techniques.

Garden Bed 1

Using two strands of 3688 together with one strand of 3689, work approximately 24 knots evenly spaced throughout the area. Then, 3689 and 3688 singly, scatter about 15 knots between those already worked. Fill the remaining spaces with 3689, then work some 523 through the flowers.

Garden Bed 2

Using two strands of 3747 together with one strand of 340, work approximately 10-12 knots in each section. Work approximately 20-25 knots using one strand of 3747 blended with one strand of ecru. Fill most of the remaining area with 3747. Finish each bed by scattering about 15 knots each of 778 and 523 through the knots previously worked.

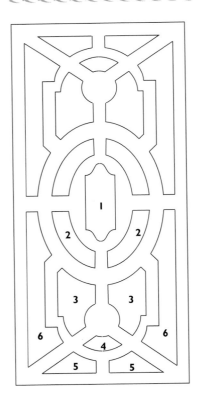

Garden Bed 3
Using one strand of 3688 blended with one strand of 3689, work approximately 20-25 knots. Fill the remaining area with 3689 and some 523.

Garden Bed 4
Fill these beds with an equal number of knots in 744 and 745, with an occasional 523.

Garden Bed 5
Fill about half the area with 3756. Fill the remaining space with 3747. Finish by scattering through some 523 and about six knots of 778 through the flowers already worked.

Garden Bed 6
Fill the area with an equal number of knots in 819, 3747, 3688, 3689 and 523.

Paths
Fill the paths with 'Blush'. Do not work the knots too densely, they should barely touch.

To finish the design, work about three rows of knots around the outer edge of the design using 523.

$\mathcal{L}$UCY'S PARTERRE GARDEN

THREADS
DMC Stranded Cotton:
316 (medium antique mauve)
335 (rose)
340 (medium blue violet)
470 (light avocado green)
471 (very light avocado green)
472 (ultra light avocado green)
524 (very light fern green)
581 (moss green)
677 (very light old gold)
734 (light olive green)
744 (pale yellow)
794 (light cornflower blue)
800 (pale delft)
819 (light baby pink)
987 (dark forest green)
3051 (dark green grey)
3345 (dark hunter green)
3346 (hunter green)
3347 (medium yellow green)
3348 (light yellow green)
3364 (pine green)
3688 (medium mauve)
3689 (light mauve)
3747 (very light blue violet)
white
Waterlilies by Caron: 'Blush'

The design is worked in single twist French Knots, with some running stitch and straight stitch. Use a single strand of thread unless otherwise specified.

Area 1
Using one strand of 3348 together with one strand of 3347, fill the circle. Work some more knots on top of those already worked, building them up in the centre to give a rounded appearance.

Using 3345, work a row of very tight knots around each circle.

Area 2
This section is divided in two. You may choose to pencil in a line.

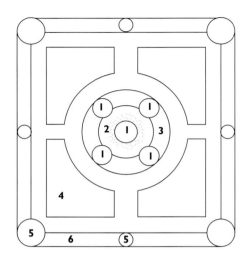

Work the shaded area first. With one strand of 819 together with one strand of 524, fill about half the area. Using 524 fill most of the remaining spaces. Scatter some 3688 through the area. Work a row of knots in 3345 around the outer edge of the flowers.

Then work the unshaded section. Using single strands of 472 and 734, fill the area with equal numbers of knots in each colour. The knots should just touch.

Area 3

Using 3347 and 3348 in single strands, fill the area with closely worked knots using more of the lighter colour. With 3345, work a tiny running stitch very close both edges of the area.

Garden Bed 4

Each bed is worked in exactly the same way. See Diagram 1 for flower placement.

Take care to leave a narrow edge around the edge of each garden bed for the white border.

(a) Using one strand of 3346 together with one strand of 3689, fill about half the area. Then, using 3689 fill any remaining spaces.

(b) Work as before using 470 and 744.

(c) Work as before using 316 and 987.

(d) Work as before using 794 and 987.

(e) Work as before using 340 and 3747.

(f) Work as before using 335 and 3364.

(g) Work as before using 677 and 471.

(h) Work as before using 800 and 3347.

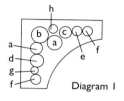

Diagram 1

To fill the spaces between the flowers, work equal numbers of knots in a single strand 734 and 581.

Complete the garden bed with a white border. Using a single strand of white, fill the whole area with closely worked knots. Then, using a single strand of 3051, scatter some very tiny straight stitches between the flowers, as described in General Techniques.

Area 5

Work as for Area 1.

Area 6

Work as for Area 3.

Paths

Fill the paths with 'Blush'. Do not work the knots too densely, they should barely touch.

$\mathcal{M}$ARY'S PARTERRE GARDEN

THREADS

Au Ver a Soie, Soie d'Alger:
2123 (very light olive green)
2125 (olive green)
DMC Stranded Cotton:
209 (dark lavender)
211 (light lavender)
340 (medium blue violet)
341(light blue violet)

543 (very light beige brown)
743 (medium yellow)
744 (pale yellow)
746 (off-white)
950 (sportsman flesh)
3746 (dark blue violet)
3747 (very light blue violet)
3770 (very light flesh)

The design is worked throughout in single twist French Knots. Use a single strand of thread unless otherwise specified.

Garden Bed 1
Outline the shape of the garden bed using equal numbers of knots in 209, 211 and 2125.

To fill the bed, work about nine knots blending one strand of 3747 with one strand of 3746. Then blend 340 and 341 and work an equal number of knots. Any remaining spaces are filled with equal numbers of knots in 209, 211 and 2125.

Garden Bed 2
Fill most of the area with 2125 and finish with three or four knots using 2123.

Garden Bed 3
Blend one strand of 743 with one strand of 744 and fill most of the bed.

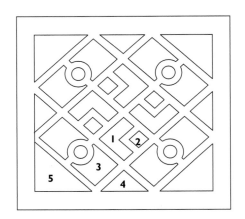

Scatter some 2123 through the flowers. Fill any remaining spaces with 746.

Garden Bed 4
Fill the area predominantly with 2125 and complete with 2123.

Garden Bed 5
Outline as for Garden Bed 1.

Blend one strand of 340 with one strand of 341 and fill a little more than half the garden. Using one strand of 3746 blended with one strand of 3747, fill most of the remaining area. Complete the section by working equal numbers of knots in 209, 211, 2125 and 3747.

Paths
Scatter some knots through the entire area using 950. Fill the remaining path areas with equal numbers of knots in 543 and 3770.

$\mathcal{K}$ATHERINE'S PARTERRE GARDEN

THREADS
Au Ver a Soie, Soie d'Alger:
white
532 (pale lemon)
536 (gold)

542 (lemon)
2123 (light pine green)
2125 (medium pine green)
2126 (pine green)
Waterlilies by Caron: 'Eggshell'

The design is worked throughout in single twist French Knots. Use a single strand of thread unless otherwise specified.

Area 1

Using one strand of 2126 blended with one strand of 2125, fill the area. Scatter some two-strand white knots on top of those already worked.

Garden Bed 2

Using first 2123, then white, work equal numbers of knots in each colour to fill most of the area. Fill any remaining area with 536.

Garden Bed 3

As described in General Techniques, outline the shape of the garden bed using 2123.

Using 2126, fill the circle in the centre of the area with knots and then work several layers of knots on top of those already worked, to build up the circle and give a domed appearance. Refer to photograph for placement.

Using 536, work three evenly spaced clusters of knots. Then with 542, scatter about five small clusters of knots through the area. With 2126, work one or two tiny straight stitches, as described in General

Techniques, through the dark yellow clusters. Then, using 2125, work about five knots scattered at random through the area. Scatter some 2123 knots through the garden bed. Fill any remaining spaces with 532.

Garden Bed 4
Using one strand of 536 blended with one strand of 542, work a row of knots following the curve of the garden bed. Refer to photograph for placement. Using 2126, work some green knots between the 'flowers' just worked.

Fill the remaining area with 2123.

Paths
Fill the paths with 'Eggshell'. Do not work the knots too densely, they should barely touch.

ALISON'S PARTERRE GARDEN

THREADS

DMC Stranded Cotton:

209 (dark lavender)
211 (light lavender)
351 (coral)
352 (light coral)
353 (peach flesh)
470 (light avocado green)
471 (light avocado green)
472 (very light avocado green)
543 (very light beige brown)
553 (violet)
554 (light violet)
603 (cranberry)
604 (light cranberry)
718 (plum)
726 (light topaz)

727 (very light topaz)
739 (very light tan)
741 (medium tangerine)
744 (pale yellow)
745 (light yellow)
746 (off white)
760 (salmon)
783 (medium topaz)
819 (light baby pink)
948 (very light peach flesh)
3328 (dark salmon)
3608 (very light plum)
3609 (ultra light plum)
3713 (very light salmon)
3746 (dark blue violet)
3747 (very light blue violet)
white

The design is worked throughout in single twist French Knots, with some running stitch. Use a single strand of thread unless otherwise specified.

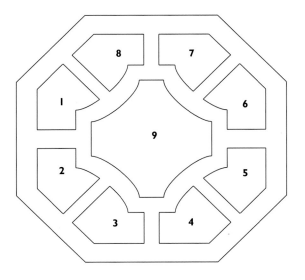

Garden Bed Borders

First, work the borders of the garden beds. You may choose to pencil in a line to mark the border areas.

All the borders are worked in the same way. Using white, outline the shape of the Garden Beds 1 to 8 as described in General Techniques. Then work about three rows of knots massed closely together inside the outline. With 471, work very small running stitches around the outside of the bed, very close to the knots.

Outline the shape of Garden Bed 9 as above, using 470. Fill approximately three-quarters of the area with equal numbers of knots in 470, 471 and 472. Fill the remaining spaces with white knots.

Garden Bed 1

Blend one strand of 741 with one strand of 744 and work seven clusters of three knots. Then, using one strand of 744 blended with one strand of 745, add three more knots to each cluster. With 471, add small groups of knots around each 'flower'. Using the same thread combinations, scatter three or four 'flowers' in Garden Bed 9. Fill any spaces in Garden 1, with knots in 746.

Garden Bed 2

Work as for Garden Bed 1, blending one strand of 353 with one strand of 351, then 352 with 353. Add three or four 'flowers' to Garden 9. Work small groups of knots in 471 around each 'flower', then fill any small spaces with 948.

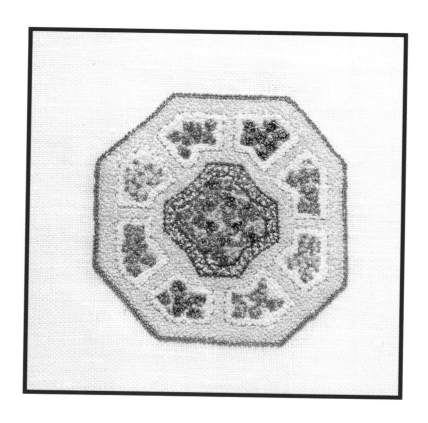

Garden Bed 3

Work as for Garden Bed 1, blending one strand of 553 with one strand of 554, then 554 with 211. Add 471 around each 'flower' as before, then fill any small spaces with equal numbers of knots in 211 and 746.

Garden Bed 4

Work as for Garden Bed 1, blending one strand of 603 with one strand of 604, then 604 with 819. Add 471 around each 'flower' as before, then fill any small spaces with knots 819.

Garden Bed 5

Work as for Garden Bed 1, blending one strand of 783 with one strand of 726, then 726 with 727. Add 471 around each 'flower' as before, then fill any small spaces with 746.

Garden Bed 6

Work as for Garden Bed 1, blending one strand of 3328 with one strand of 760, then using two strands of 760. Add 471 around each 'flower' as before, then fill any small spaces with equal numbers of knots in 3713 and 746.

Garden Bed 7

Work as for Garden Bed 1, blending one strand of 3746 with one strand of 3747, then blending 209 with 211. Add 471 around each 'flower' as before, then fill any small spaces with equal numbers of knots in 3747 and 746.

Garden Bed 8

Work as for Garden Bed 1, blending one strand of 3608 with one strand of 718, then 3608 with 3609. Add 471 around each 'flower' as before, then fill any small spaces with 819.

Garden Bed 9

Fill any remaining small spaces between the 'flowers' with knots using 746, 819, 948 or 3747 in any combination.

Paths

Fill the paths with knots using equal numbers of 739 and 543. Do not work the knots too densely, they should barely touch.

Optional

You may choose to add two rows of knots using 471 around the outer edge of the design.

. . . .

Flowers that their gay wardrobe wear.

MILTON

．．．．．．．．．．．．．．．．．

What was Paradise?
But a garden, full of pleasure,
And nothing there but delight.

LAWSON

．．．．．．．．．．．．．．．．．

And 'tis my faith that every flower
Enjoys the air it breathes.

WORDSWORTH

She said that she would dance with me if I brought her red roses.

OSCAR WILDE

Earth laughs in flowers.

EMERSON